BIGGEST NAMES IN SPORTS

JA MORANT

BASKETBALL STAR

by Hubert Walker

FOCUS READERS.

NAVIGATOR

WWW.FOCUSREADERS.COM

Focus Readers is distributed by North Star Editions:
sales@northstareditions.com | 888-417-0195

Produced for Focus Readers by Red Line Editorial.

Photographs ©: Brandon Dill/AP Images, cover, 1, 7, 8, 26; Joe Murphy/NBAE/National Basketball Association/Getty Images, 4–5; Stephen Furst/Icon Sportswire/AP Images, 10–11, 13; Ryan Hermens/The Paducah Sun/AP Images, 15; Ellen O'Nan/The Paducah Sun/AP Images, 16–17; Elise Amendola/AP Images, 19; Julio Cortez/AP Images, 21; Karen Pulfer Focht/AP Images, 22–23; Nikki Boertman/AP Images, 25; Red Line Editorial, 29

Library of Congress Cataloging-in-Publication Data
Names: Walker, Hubert, 1980- author.
Title: Ja Morant : basketball star / by Hubert Walker.
Description: Lake Elmo, MN : Focus Readers, 2021. | Series: Biggest names in sports | Includes index. | Audience: Grades 4-6
Identifiers: LCCN 2020033626 (print) | LCCN 2020033627 (ebook) | ISBN 9781644937020 (hardcover) | ISBN 9781644937389 (paperback) | ISBN 9781644938102 (pdf) | ISBN 9781644937747 (ebook)
Subjects: LCSH: Morant, Ja--Juvenile literature. | Basketball players--United States--Biography--Juvenile literature. | African American basketball players--Biography--Juvenile literature.
Classification: LCC GV884.M638 W35 2021 (print) | LCC GV884.M638 (ebook) | DDC 796.323092 [B]--dc23
LC record available at https://lccn.loc.gov/2020033626
LC ebook record available at https://lccn.loc.gov/2020033627

Printed in the United States of America
Mankato, MN
012023

ABOUT THE AUTHOR

Hubert Walker enjoys running, hunting, and going to the dog park with his best pal. He grew up in Georgia but moved to Minnesota in 2018. Overall, he loves his new home, but he's not a fan of the cold winters.

TABLE OF CONTENTS

CHAPTER 1

Sending a Message 5

CHAPTER 2

Overlooked 11

CHAPTER 3

Sophomore Star 17

CHAPTER 4

Rookie Sensation 23

At-a-Glance Map • 28

Focus on Ja Morant • 30

Glossary • 31

To Learn More • 32

Index • 32

SENDING A MESSAGE

Ja Morant dribbled the ball to the top of the three-point arc. Morant and the Memphis Grizzlies were facing off against the Houston Rockets during a 2019–20 regular-season game. Rockets superstar James Harden guarded Morant from several feet away. Harden almost seemed to be daring the **rookie** to shoot.

Ja Morant (right) drives past James Harden during a 2020 game between the Memphis Grizzlies and the Houston Rockets.

Morant didn't hesitate. He pulled up for a long jump shot and splashed in a three-pointer. The young point guard roared with excitement as he hustled back on defense.

It can be hard for a rookie to get respect from **veteran** players. It can be even harder to get respect from a superstar like Harden. But Morant showed he could take on one of the best players in the game. And his night was just getting started.

In the second quarter, Morant drove hard toward the basket. Two defenders quickly stepped up to guard him. But Morant dished off a behind-the-back pass

Morant heaves a pass to a teammate during a 2020 game against the Rockets.

to Jaren Jackson Jr. The Grizzlies forward scored an easy basket.

Later in the quarter, Morant drove toward the basket again. This time, only one defender stood in his way. Morant dribbled past him with an incredible

Morant looks to shoot during a 2020 game against the Rockets.

spin move. Then he finished off the play with a quick layup.

As the half was winding down, Morant brought the ball down the court. Harden reached in to attempt a steal. But Morant dribbled behind his back and blew right past Harden. Next, Morant jumped up to make a cross-court pass. In midair, he spotted teammate Brandon Clarke leaping toward the basket. Morant delivered a quick pass to Clarke, who slammed home the alley-oop. The Memphis crowd went wild.

Morant finished the game with an impressive 26 points, 8 **assists**, and 5 rebounds. He helped the Grizzlies cruise to a 121–110 victory.

Morant sent a powerful message to the rest of the National Basketball Association (NBA). He wasn't afraid to compete with the league's biggest superstars. And he was well on his way to becoming a superstar himself.

OVERLOOKED

Temetrius Jamel Morant was born on August 10, 1999. His nickname, Ja, comes from the first two letters of his middle name. Ja grew up in the small town of Dalzell, South Carolina. Both of his parents were athletes. His father played basketball semiprofessionally. His mother played softball in college.

Morant started shooting hoops when he was just two years old.

As a kid, Ja spent hours practicing basketball with his dad. He developed excellent skills. But all through middle school, Ja was short. Fortunately, he hit a growth spurt in high school. By the time Ja was a junior, he stood 6 feet (1.8 m) tall. And he was still growing.

Ja established himself as the leader of his high school basketball team. He put up huge numbers. In his junior year, he averaged 27 points per game. However, despite his impressive stats, big-name colleges didn't show any interest in him.

Ja felt frustrated, but he kept at it. He wanted to prove that he could play at a high level. Later in the year, Murray State

Morant makes a move to the basket during a 2017 Murray State game.

University offered him a **scholarship**. Murray State wasn't a big-name school. Even so, Ja liked the coaches. He accepted the school's offer.

Morant began his freshman year of college in 2017. He had a solid season with the Murray State Racers, averaging 12.7 points per game. However, he was not the star of the team. Morant played a supporting role. Older, more experienced players did most of the scoring.

SURPRISING DISCOVERY

In 2016, a **scout** from Murray State attended a **combine** for high school players. The combine's best-known players were in the building's main gym. At one point, the scout left the main gym to buy a bag of chips. He overheard a game taking place in a smaller gym. He looked inside. There, he saw Ja Morant playing three-on-three. The scout was blown away. Days later, Murray State offered Ja a scholarship.

Morant goes for a layup during a 2018 game against Austin Peay State University.

After his freshman season, Morant began spending more time in the weight room. He also put in more hours on the practice court. By the time his sophomore year rolled around, Morant was ready to be a leader.

SOPHOMORE STAR

Few people knew Ja Morant at the start of his sophomore year. But that soon changed. During the 2018–19 season, Morant took the National Collegiate Athletic Association (NCAA) by storm. He became a one-man highlight reel. His monster dunks and incredible passes forced the basketball world to take notice.

Morant powers through a defender during his sophomore year at Murray State.

Fans raved about Morant's amazing **vision** on the court. He seemed to know exactly where his teammates would be. He also saw passing opportunities that other players didn't. With skills like that, it was no surprise that Morant led the NCAA in assists.

BEST OF THE BEST

Morant's 2018–19 season was one for the record books. He averaged more than 20 points and 10 rebounds that season. He was the first player in NCAA history to do that. Morant was also a First Team All-American. In addition, he won the Bob Cousy Award. This award is given to the best point guard in the NCAA.

Morant dunks on a Marquette player during the first round of the 2019 NCAA tournament.

After the regular season ended, Murray State faced Marquette in the NCAA tournament. Basketball experts didn't expect the Racers to win. But Morant was on fire. Early in the second half, he electrified the crowd with a powerful two-handed dunk. Seconds later, he hauled in a rebound. Then he sent a long pass to teammate Tevin Brown, who scored on a fast break. Morant notched a **triple-double** in the game. Best of all, he led his team to a blowout victory.

Murray State came up short in the second round of the tournament. But even in the loss, Morant racked up 28 points. Less than two weeks later, Morant announced that he was ending his college career. He planned to enter the 2019 NBA **Draft**.

The draft took place in June 2019. The New Orleans Pelicans had the first pick. They selected Zion Williamson.

Morant poses for a picture with NBA commissioner Adam Silver after being drafted by the Memphis Grizzlies.

Then, with the second pick, the Memphis Grizzlies chose Morant. The 19-year-old walked onstage. He put on his new Grizzlies cap. Even though the big-name colleges had ignored him, Morant was heading to the NBA.

ROOKIE SENSATION

When Ja Morant joined the Grizzlies, he became part of a struggling team. Memphis hadn't reached the playoffs in the past two seasons. Grizzlies fans hoped Morant would be the spark that the team needed.

By the season's third game, Morant had proved that he was ready to take

Morant dribbles downcourt during a 2019 game against the Los Angeles Lakers.

on that role. Facing the Brooklyn Nets, Morant scored the tying basket with just seven seconds left. Nets guard Kyrie Irving attempted a game-winning shot as the clock ticked down to zero. But Morant swatted the ball away. In overtime, Morant came up big again. The Grizzlies

BIRTHDAY GIFT

Morant turned 20 years old in August 2019. To celebrate his birthday, he decided to help his community. He urged fans to donate money to the Boys & Girls Club of Greater Memphis. This group helps young people learn skills that can help them later in life. Morant promised to match the donations that fans made.

Morant throws down a huge dunk during a 2019 game against the Cleveland Cavaliers.

trailed by two points with three seconds remaining. Morant dribbled down the court. Then he passed the ball to Jae Crowder. The Grizzlies forward nailed a three-pointer to win the game.

Morant delivers a pass past Mo Bamba of the Orlando Magic during a March 2020 game.

Morant dazzled fans in game after game. He became famous for his energetic dunks and no-look passes. But he knew there was still room for improvement. For example, Morant wasn't as strong as most players in the league.

Working on his strength would help him defend better. He also didn't attempt many three-point shots. Sinking more threes would help his team score more points. Morant was determined to get even better. And that was a scary thought for opposing teams.

Morant's hard work paid off. In 2021, he led Memphis to the playoffs. However, the Grizzlies lost in the first round. The loss was disappointing. But the next season, Morant played better than ever. He made his first All-Star Game. Memphis also reached the second round of the playoffs. Grizzlies fans hoped that a trip to the Finals was soon to come.

JA MORANT

- Height: 6 feet 3 inches (191 cm)
- Weight: 175 pounds (79 kg)
- Birth date: August 10, 1999
- Birthplace: Dalzell, South Carolina
- High school: Crestwood High School (Sumter, South Carolina)
- College: Murray State University (Murray, Kentucky) (2017–2019)
- NBA team: Memphis Grizzlies (2019–)
- Major awards: All-America First Team (2019); Bob Cousy Award (2019); NBA Rookie of the Year (2020); NBA All-Star (2022)

FOCUS ON
JA MORANT

Write your answers on a separate piece of paper.

1. Write a paragraph that explains the main ideas of Chapter 2.

2. Do you think Morant's career would have been different if he had gone to a big-name college? Why or why not?

3. Which player was chosen before Morant in the 2019 NBA Draft?

> **A.** Zion Williamson
> **B.** James Harden
> **C.** Kyrie Irving

4. Which skill helps Morant rack up assists?

> **A.** dribbling
> **B.** vision
> **C.** dunking

Answer key on page 32.

GLOSSARY

assists
Passes that lead directly to a teammate scoring a basket.

combine
An event in which athletes show off their skills to scouts.

draft
A system that allows teams to acquire new players coming into a league.

rookie
A professional athlete in his or her first year.

scholarship
Money given to a student to pay for education expenses.

scout
A person who looks for talented young players.

triple-double
A game in which a player has double-digit numbers in three categories, often points, assists, and rebounds.

veteran
A person who has been doing his or her job for a long time and has a lot of experience.

vision
The ability to see what is happening during a game and to understand where other players will be as a play develops.

TO LEARN MORE

BOOKS

Mahoney, Brian. *Basketball's New Wave: The Young Superstars Taking Over the Game*. Burnsville, MN: Press Room Editions, 2019.

Savage, Jeff. *Basketball Super Stats*. Minneapolis: Lerner Publications, 2017.

Smibert, Angie. *STEM in Basketball*. Minneapolis: Abdo Publishing, 2018.

NOTE TO EDUCATORS

Visit **www.focusreaders.com** to find lesson plans, activities, links, and other resources related to this title.

INDEX

Bob Cousy Award, 18
Boys & Girls Club of Greater Memphis, 24
Brooklyn Nets, 24
Brown, Tevin, 20

Clarke, Brandon, 9
Crowder, Jae, 25

Dalzell, South Carolina, 11

First Team All-American, 18

Harden, James, 5–6, 8
Houston Rockets, 5

Irving, Kyrie, 24

Jackson, Jaren, Jr., 7

Marquette University, 19
Memphis Grizzlies, 5, 7, 9, 21, 23–25, 27
Murray State University, 12–14, 19, 20

National Collegiate Athletic Association (NCAA), 17–19
NBA Draft, 20–21
New Orleans Pelicans, 20

playoffs, 23, 27

Williamson, Zion, 20